Pocket Pilot:

Your Go To Guide for Drone Flying Success

By: AMANDA OTIS

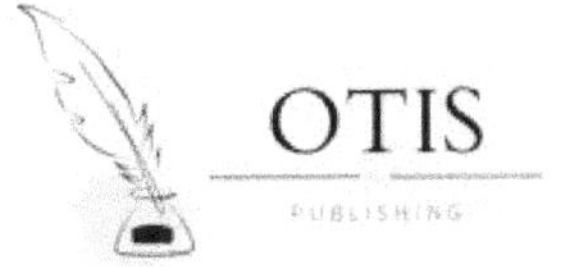

Contents

Introduction

Welcome to "Pocket Pilot: Your Go-To Guide for Drone Flying Success"!

Regardless of whether you're just launching into the world of drones or looking to sharpen your flight skills, this compact guide is designed to be your trusted co-pilot every step of the way. Flying a drone is more than just pushing a few buttons—it's a blend of skill, responsibility, and creativity. And with the rapid rise in recreational and commercial drone use, understanding the rules of the sky, mastering your equipment, and staying safe have never been more important.

This guide was created to be practical, easy to navigate, and packed with essential tips, checklists, and insights—perfect for slipping into your backpack or glove box. You'll find simplified FAA regulations, quick-reference charts, weather guidelines, flight planning tips, safety protocols, and even photography advice for capturing those breathtaking aerial views.

Whether you're aiming to pass the FAA Part 107 exam, planning your first scenic flight, or building your skills as a drone photographer or videographer, *Pocket Pilot* gives you the confidence to fly smart, stay compliant, and have fun doing it.

So power up, take off, and let's explore the skies—safely, skillfully, and successfully.

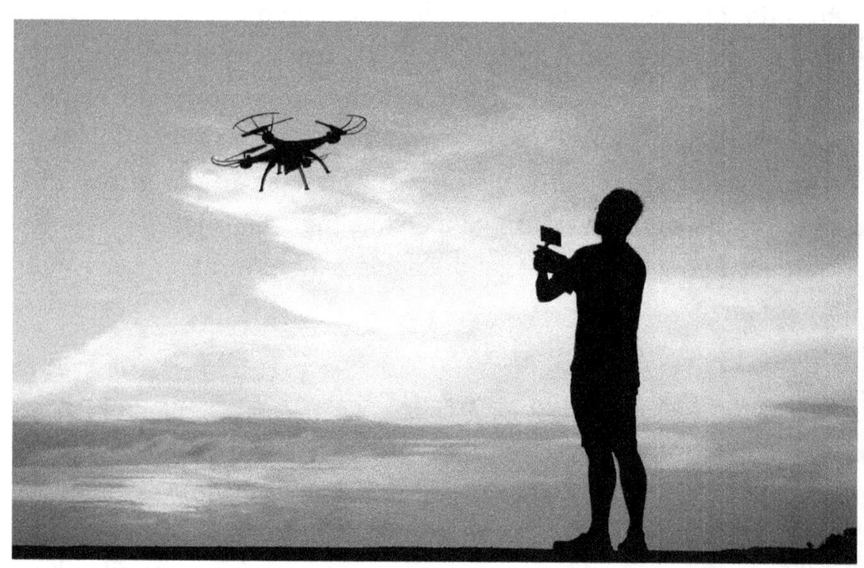

Chapter 1: Legal Requirements

Flying a drone in the United States—especially for photography—requires understanding and following federal regulations established by the Federal Aviation Administration (FAA). Whether you're capturing family portraits from above or shooting landscapes for commercial use, staying compliant helps protect airspace safety and keeps your flights legal and worry-free.

Register Your Drone

All drones that weigh more than 0.55 pounds (250 grams) and less than 55 pounds must be registered with the FAA, even for recreational use. You can register online through the FAA DroneZone website. Once registered, you'll receive a unique registration number that must be visibly labeled on the outside of your drone. Registration is valid for three years.

Know the Difference: Recreational vs. Commercial Use

• Recreational Use: If you're flying strictly for fun and not making money from your photography, you must follow the rules of the Exception for Recreational Flyers, sometimes called the Section 44809 rules.

• Commercial Use: If you intend to use your drone photography for business purposes—such as selling photos, doing real estate work, or using footage for marketing—you must have a Part 107 Remote Pilot Certificate, also known as the FAA's drone license.

Get Your FAA Part 107 Certification (For Commercial Flyers)

To fly legally for commercial photography, you must pass the FAA's Part 107 knowledge exam, which covers airspace classifications, weather, drone operation, and emergency procedures. You must be:

- At least 16 years old
- Able to read, write, and speak English
- In physical and mental condition to safely operate a drone

Once certified, you must carry your certificate when flying and complete recurring training every 24 months.

Follow FAA Operational Rules

No matter your purpose, all drone pilots must follow these basic guidelines:

- Fly below 400 feet AGL (Above Ground Level)
- Keep your drone within visual line of sight
- Don't fly over people or moving vehicles (unless you have proper

waivers or your drone meets specific safety categories)
· Don't fly at night unless your drone has appropriate lighting
· Avoid flying near airports or in controlled air space unless you have FAA authorization (via LAANC or DroneZone)

Respect Local and State Laws

In addition to federal regulations, some states and cities have their own drone laws, especially concerning privacy, flying over private property, or local park restrictions. Always check local ordinances before launching.

Understanding and following these legal requirements helps protect your rights as a responsible drone pilot and ensures you can keep flying — and photographing—safely and legally.

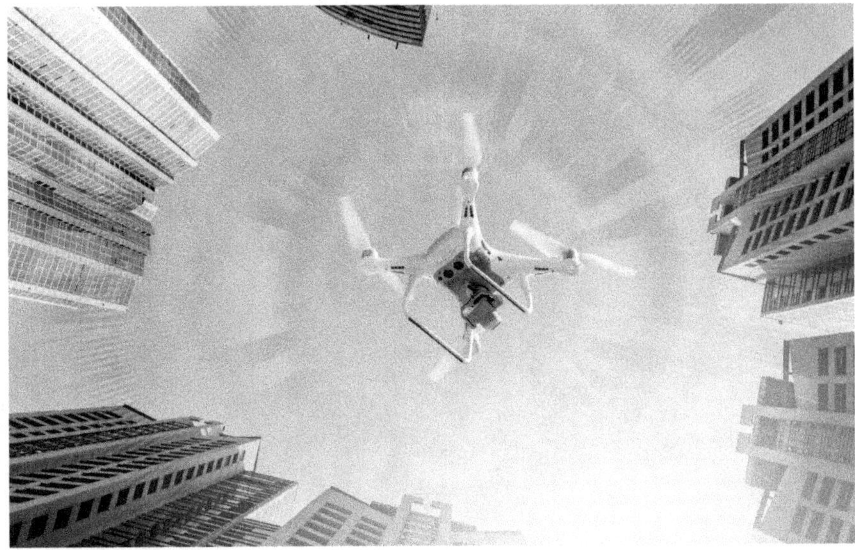

Chapter 2: Flight Safety Guidelines

Drone flying is an exciting hobby and a valuable professional tool, but with that freedom comes responsibility. Ensuring flight safety is not just about avoiding accidents—it's about protecting airspace, respecting privacy, complying with federal regulations, and fostering public trust in drone operations. Whether you're new to drones or already certified, reviewing safety best practices before every flight is essential.

The Basics of Flight Safety

Before every takeoff, there are a few golden rules that every drone operator in the United States should follow. The FAA provides clear guidelines to help ensure drones are operated safely and legally. These include:

- Flight Safety Guidelines
- Maximum Altitude: 400 feet above ground level(AGL) in the U.S.
- Maintain line of sight (no flying beyond visual range).
- Avoid flying near people, animals, or property.
- Maintain at least 5 miles distance from airports unless cleared by

ATC.

· Follow the "don't fly over people" rule unless properly authorized.

Let's break down what each of these means in practice and how you can implement them in your flying routine.

Maximum Altitude: 400 Feet AGL

The 400-foot rule exists to minimize the risk of collision with manned aircraft, which typically fly at higher altitudes. Always monitor your drone's altitude using your controller display or app. Flying above 400 feet could put your drone in violation of FAA regulations and endanger nearby aircraft.

Pro Tip: When flying in hilly or mountainous terrain, remember that "above ground level" is measured from the point on the ground directly beneath your drone—not from your takeoff point.

Maintain Visual Line of Sight (VLOS)

Visual line of sight means you, the pilot, must be able to see your drone at all times during flight without the aid of binoculars or screens. This allows you to monitor your drone's position and respond immediately to hazards or obstacles.

Flying beyond visual range can result in loss of control, collisions, or violation of controlled airspace.

Pro Tip: Use a visual observer (VO) if you're capturing footage while focusing on your screen. The VO's job is to keep eyes on the drone at all times and communicate with you.

Avoid Flying Near People, Animals, or Property

Drones can be unpredictable—unexpected wind gusts, battery failure, or GPS loss can cause crashes. For this reason, FAA rules prohibit flying directly over people who aren't involved in your operation unless your drone meets specific safety criteria and you're authorized to do so.

Animals may react unpredictably to drone noise, and flying near homes or private property could result in privacy complaints or legal trouble.

Safe Practice: Fly in open areas such as parks (where permitted), empty fields, or designated flight zones.

Stay at Least 5 Miles from Airports

Drones can pose a serious threat to manned aircraft during takeoff or landing. The FAA requires drone pilots to avoid flying within five miles of an airport unless they receive clearance from Air Traffic Control (ATC).

For most recreational flyers, this clearance can be obtained through apps and services using the Low Altitude Authorization and Notification Capability (LAANC). For Part 107 pilots, LAANC or DroneZone can be used to apply for operational approval.

Pro Tip: Use FAA-approved drone flight apps to check for controlled airspace before flying.

Don't Fly Over People (Unless Authorized)

Flying over crowds, events, roads, or public gatherings is a serious safety risk.

The FAA allows this only under strict conditions:

- Your drone must fall into an approved Category 1–4 classification based on safety standards.
- The drone must have no exposed rotating parts that could cause injury.
- You must follow additional FAA requirements if flying at night or over moving vehicles.

Unless you've received proper training and certification—and your drone qualifies—stick to the rule: no flying over people.

Additional Flight Safety Tips

- Check the weather. Avoid flying in rain, high winds, or extreme temperatures.
- Do a pre-flight check. Inspect your drone for damage, ensure batteries are charged, calibrate your compass and GPS, and double-check camera and SD card readiness.
- Watch your battery life. Always land before your battery runs critically low.
- Respectprivacy. Avoid recording people or private property without permission.
- Have a return-to-home (RTH) plan. Most drones have an RTH feature—make sure it's programmed correctly.

As drones continue to gain popularity in recreational and commercial use, it's more important than ever to fly responsibly. Following safety rules protects not just your drone—but people, property, and the future of drone aviation as a whole.

Every responsible drone pilot is also an ambassador for the drone community. Fly smart, stay informed, and never underestimate the importance of safe skies.

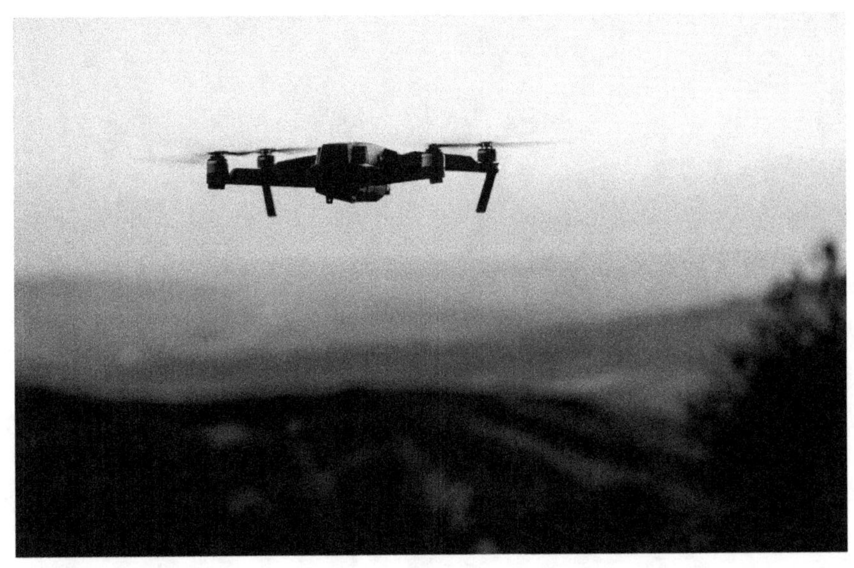

Chapter 3: Drone Controller and App Basics

Safe and successful drone operation requires more than just clear skies and a charged battery. Understanding your drone's controls and learning how to interpret the information on your controller app are essential skills for every pilot—whether you're flying recreationally or commercially.

This section will help you master the core elements of drone movement and the key data points that keep your flight safe and controlled. By getting familiar with both your physical remote and the digital app interface, you'll have the confidence to fly with precision and avoid common pitfalls.

Controller and App Basics

Let's start with the most important functions on your drone controller–the commands that govern how your drone moves in space.

Controller and App Basics
- Throttle (up/down): Controls altitude.
- Yaw (left/right): Rotates the drone.
- Pitch (forward/backward): Moves the drone forward or backward.
- Roll (left/right): Moves the drone sideways.

Key app features to monitor:
- GPS signal strength
- Battery life
- Altitude and distance from home point

Let's explore these in more depth.

Controller Stick Movements: Your Drone's Flight Language

Throttle(Up/Down):
The throttle increases or decreases the power going to your drone's motors, which affects its altitude. Pushing the left stick (on most controllers) up makes the drone ascend; pushing it down brings it closer to the ground. Smooth throttle control is essential for precise takeoffs and landings.

Yaw(Left/Right):
Yaw rotates your drone clockwise or counterclockwise, allowing

you to change the direction the drone's camera is facing without changing position. This is especially useful when framing shots or navigating tight areas.

Pitch(Forward/Backward):

Pitch moves the drone forward or backward by tilting the nose of the aircraft. This function is critical for following subjects or moving through space efficiently.

Roll(Left/Right):

Roll moves the drone sideways (laterally), ideal for tracking shots or repositioning without rotating the drone. It's useful for fine-tuning framing during flight.

Understanding Your Drone App Interface

Your drone app (such as DJI Fly, Autel Explorer, or Skydio app) is your flight dashboard. While some pilots rely solely on the controller, the app provides critical telemetry and visual feedback that enhances your awareness and flight safety.

Here are the most important features to watch during flight:

1. GPS Signal Strength

- A strong GPS lock helps maintain drone stability, enables return-to-home (RTH) functionality, and improves flight tracking.
- Poor GPS signals can lead to flyaways, unstablehovering, or drift. Avoid flying in areas with tall buildings, thick trees, or heavy interference.

2. Battery Life

- Monitor your battery percentage and estimated flight time remaining closely.
- Most apps offer low battery warnings and auto-return-to-home settings—make sure these are enabled and tested.
- Never push your drone to the last few percent of battery. Always aim to land before your battery dips below 20–25%.

3. Altitude and Distance from Home Point

- Know your drone's altitude relative to ground level (AGL) to stay under the legal 400 ft. limit in the U.S.
- Keep an eye on distance from your takeoff point (home point), especially in windy or line-of-sight-limited situations.
- If your drone gets too far, GPS-based return-to-home (RTH) features can help bring it back, but they rely on accurate data.

Why This Knowledge Matters for Safety

A large number of drone incidents happen because the pilot didn't understand how to control the drone or misread the information on their app. Whether you're capturing footage or just learning to fly, a few mistakes can result in crashes, lost drones, or even FAA violations.

Scenarios Where These Skills Save the Day:

- Strong wind warning: You notice your drone struggling to return, and quickly use pitch and throttle to safely descend and fly closer.

- Low GPS signal: Instead of relying on GPS stabilization, you smoothly control your drone using manual throttle, yaw, and roll to bring it back.
- Battery drops rapidly: By watching your app and understanding your return range, you avoid a crash or forced auto-landing.

Pro Tips for Safe, Controlled Flying

- Practice flight movements individually before combining them for complex maneuvers.
- Use a simulator app or beginner mode (if your drone has one) to build confidence.
- Always calibrate your compass and check IMU status before flying in a new location.
- Perform test flights in wide open spaces before using your drone on professional jobs.

Fly Smart, Stay in Control

Knowing how to use your controller and drone app isn't just about convenience—it's about safety. Clear control of your drone means less stress, fewer accidents, and more successful flights. Take the time to practice, stay familiar with your drone's interface, and always keep an eye on key metrics during your flight.

Chapter 4: No-Fly Zones and Airspace Classifications

Flying a drone offers breathtaking views and incredible creative potential, but it also comes with a serious responsibility: knowing where you can and can't fly. Violating airspace restrictions can result in fines, loss of your drone, or even legal consequences. Whether you're a hobbyist or commercial drone pilot, understanding no-fly zones and airspace classifications is a foundational part of safe and legal drone operation.

Why Airspace Rules Matter

Airspace in the United States is tightly regulated by the Federal Aviation Administration (FAA) to keep manned and unmanned aircraft safe. Drones share the skies with airplanes, helicopters, emergency aircraft, and military flights—so proper coordination and adherence to airspace rules are essential.

Flying in the wrong place—especially near airports or government facilities—not only endangers lives but could also put you in violation of federal law.

Classified Airspace: What You Need to Know

The airspace in the U.S. is divided into different classes. As a drone pilot, you're most likely to encounter Classes B, C, D, and E, which are controlled airspace—meaning flights within these areas typically require prior FAA authorization.

Class B Airspace

Surrounds the nation's busiest airports (e.g., LAX, JFK, ORD). Extends from the ground up to 10,000 feet in a layered "upside-down wedding cake" structure.

FAA authorization is mandatory. Drone operations are rarely approved near Class B airspace unless for commercial use with a waiver.

Class C Airspace

Found around smaller commercial airports. Requires authorization through tools like LAANC (Low Altitude Authorization and Notification Capability). Often extends 5 nautical miles from the airport and from the surface up to 4,000 feet AGL.

Class D Airspace

Typically surrounds small airports with an operational control tower. Surface area extends about 4–5 miles from the airport. Drone pilots must obtain FAA clearance, but it's commonly granted via LAANC or FAA Drone Zone.

Class E Airspace

Controlled airspace that begins at varying altitudes (often 700 or 1,200 feet AGL) and extends upward. Most drone operations don't take place in Class E airspace unless you fly above 400 feet, which is not permitted without FAA authorization.

Restricted and Prohibited Areas

Beyond controlled airspace, there are areas that are completely off-limits or heavily restricted, regardless of altitude or purpose.

National Parks

The National Park Service (NPS) bans drone flights in all U.S. national parks unless you have a special permit. Violating this rule can lead to steep fines and drone confiscation.

Military Bases and Government Facilities

Many military bases, weapons testing areas, and sensitive government installations (like the White House or power plants) are located in Special Use Airspace (SUA). These areas are often labeled as Restricted, Prohibited, or Military Operation Areas (MOAs). These zones are legally enforced and often use signal jammers or GPS spoofing to bring down unauthorized drones.

Temporary Flight Restrictions (TFRs)

These are issued for emergencies, public events, VIP movements (like the President), or natural disasters. Always check for TFRs before you fly. They change frequently and are strictly enforced.

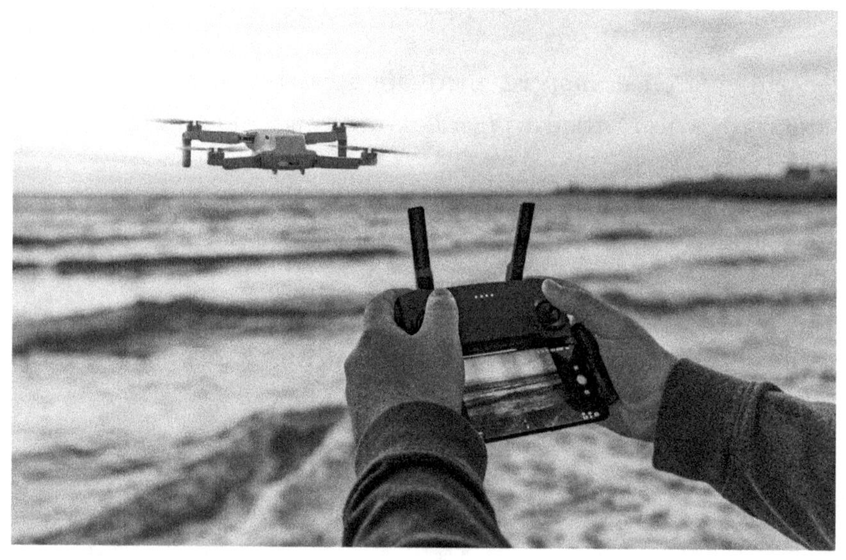

Use Apps to Stay Safe and Legal

The FAA recommends using trusted, color-coded map apps to stay aware of airspace classifications and no-fly zones.

Some of the most helpful apps for drone pilots include:

- B4UFLY (by the FAA): Great for hobbyists. Shows TFRs, controlled airspace, and local advisories.
- Aloft (formerly Kittyhawk): Offers LAANC requests and real-time airspace info.
- AirMap: Used for airspace planning, real-time airspace alerts, and authorization submissions.
- DroneDeploy & Skyward: Professional mapping and flight planning tools that integrate with airspace data.

Color-coding makes it easy:

- Red zones: No-fly areas (e.g., restricted airspace, TFRs).
- Yellow/orange zones: Controlled airspace that may require FAA approval
- Green zones: Uncontrolled airspace where flying is allowed (still subject to basic rules)

Best Practices for Safe Flight Planning

To avoid running afoul of airspace restrictions:

· Always check the airspace before you fly—even for short, recreational flights.
· Submit authorization requests via LAANC or FAA DroneZone for controlled airspace.
· Respect all signage and park rules — if it says "NoDroneZone," take it seriously.
· Keep records of your flight plans and authorizations, especially if flying commercially.
· Never fly near airports, emergency scenes, or stadiums without proper clearance.

Consequences of Violating No-Fly Zones

Penalties for violating airspace rules can include:

· Civil fines up to $32,666 per violation.
· Criminal charges if safety is compromised or national security is threatened.
· Confiscation of your drone and potential revocation of your Part 107 certification.

Knowledge = Safety and Success

Understanding airspace classifications and where you can safely fly is one of the most important responsibilities you carry as a drone pilot. It ensures the safety of manned aviation, protects sensitive locations, and helps you avoid fines or worse.

Respecting airspace isn't just about obeying the law—it's about being a responsible part of the drone community and keeping the skies safe for everyone.

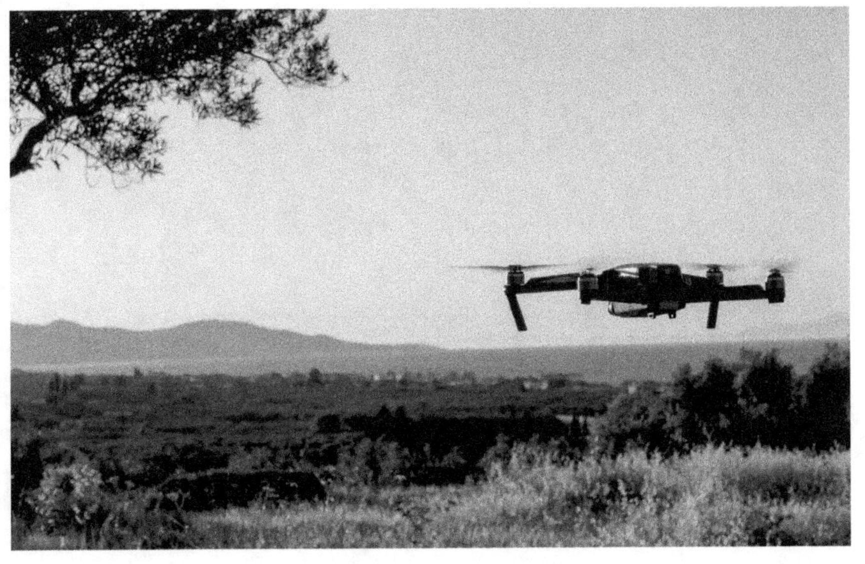

Chapter 5: Weather and Environmental Safety

Weather is one of the most critical factors to consider before launching your drone. Unlike larger aircraft, drones are lightweight, battery- powered, and highly sensitive to environmental conditions. Even experienced pilots can lose control when the weather turns unfavorable. That's why being weather-aware is a fundamental part of responsible and safe drone flight.

Wind Speed and Gusts

Wind is one of the most underestimated hazards in drone operations. Strong gusts can easily throw your drone off course, drain the battery faster, or even cause crashes. While some high-end drones can handle moderate breezes, the ideal wind speed is below 15 mph for safe and stable flight. If you're a beginner or flying a lightweight drone, aim for even calmer conditions—under 10 mph is best.

Always check for gust speed as well. Sudden gusts can be more dangerous than steady winds, especially when flying at higher altitudes or in open areas like fields or coastlines.

Rain, Fog, and Snow

Moisture is a drone's worst enemy. Most consumer drones are not waterproof or even water-resistant. Avoid flying in rain, fog, or snow to prevent internal component damage, GPS malfunctions, or signal interference.

Fog also reduces visibility, making it harder to maintain line of sight—a legal requirement in most cases—and increasing the risk of collisions with unseen objects like power lines, trees, or buildings.

High Temperatures and Battery Health

Flying in hot weather presents its own set of risks. Be cautious of high temperatures that can overheat batteries. Overheating can shorten battery lifespan, reduce flight time, and in extreme cases, lead to battery failure or even fire.

Avoid flying during peak sun hours on extremely hot days, and always let your batteries cool before recharging. Store them in a shaded, ventilated area and use a fireproof LiPo bag for added safety.

Weather Planning Tips

• Use drone-specific weather apps like UAV Forecast, Hover, or Windy to check conditions.
• Look for real-time data on wind, visibility, precipitation, and cloud cover.
• Postpone your flight if any adverse weather conditions are present or expected.
• Performapre-flight checklist that includes inspecting the drone for condensation, dirt, or debris from past flights.

Understanding and respecting weather conditions can prevent accidents, protect your equipment, and ensure a smoother flying experience. Always remember: just because the sky looks clear doesn't mean it's safe to fly. A responsible drone pilot checks the weather every time — and knows when to stay grounded.

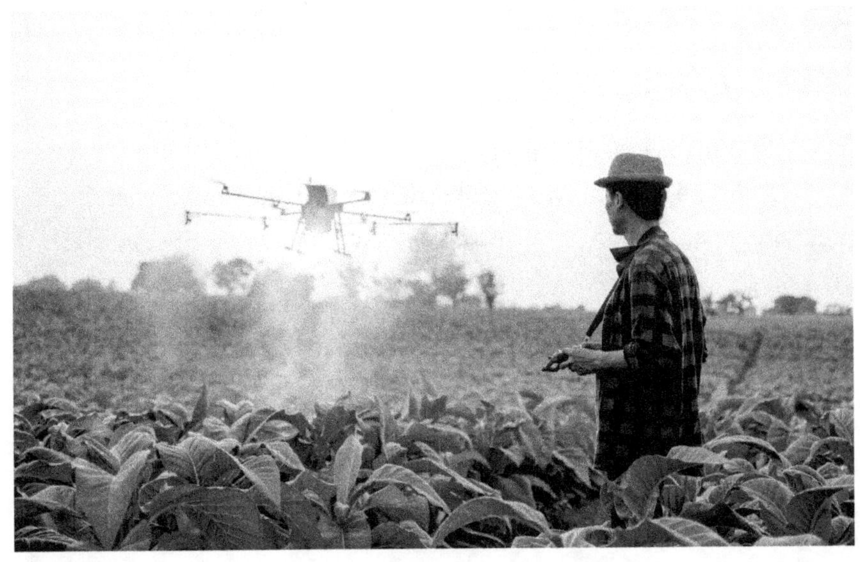

Drone Flight Weather & Environmental Safety Checklist

Weather Conditions

___ Wind speed is below 15 mph

___ No gusts exceeding safelimits for your drone model

___ No rain, snow, or fog in the area

___ Temperature is within safe operating range (typically 32°F to 95°F)

___ UV index and sunglare are manageable (wear polarized sunglasses if needed)

Temperature and Battery Precautions

___ Batteries are not overheating before flight

___ Batteries were stored at room temperature

___ Avoid flying during peak midday heat in summer

___ Cold weather flights: batteries are fully charged and warm

Visibility & Line of Sight

___ Visibility is at least 3 miles

___ Clear line of sight with no obstructions (trees,buildings,etc.)

___ Sun position won't cause loss of visual tracking

Environmental Hazards

___ Area is free of birds, wildlife, or large crowds

___ Note all obstacles (powerlines, antennas, cranes, etc.)

___ Flying surface is flat and safe for take off/landing

___ Avoid flying over bodies of water unless trained and insured

Technology & Tools

___ GPS signal is strong
___ Weather checked via UAV Forecast, Windy,or local apps
___ No unexpected magnetic interference (check compass calibration)

Pro Tip: If more than one item on this list isn't checked, reconsider flying or delay until conditions improve.

NOTES

____

____

____

____

____

____

____

____

____

____

Chapter 6: Pre-Flight Procedures

Flying a drone is more than just powering it on and taking to the skies. It requires planning, awareness, and technical readiness. A solid pre-flight procedure ensures your drone is safe to fly, protects your equipment, and reduces the risk of violating airspace regulations or encountering mid-air issues.

Whether you're capturing cinematic footage, mapping land, or flying recreationally, pre-flight preparation lays the groundwork for success.

Why Pre-Flight Procedures Matter

Even the most experienced drone pilots benefit from following a consistent pre-flight routine.

Why? Because:

- Environmental factors change— wind, visibility, and nearby obstacles can vary.
- Technology evolves—firmware updates, GPS connectivity, and app changes can affect functionality.
- Regulations apply—knowing where and when you're allowed to fly is essential to staying legal.

Overlooking even one small detail—like failing to calibrate your compass or check wind conditions—can lead to unexpected crashes, lost drones, or legal trouble.

Preparation Begins Before You Fly

Start your pre-flight planning at home or in the office before ever heading to your launch site. Use apps like B4UFLY, AirMap, or DroneDeploy to verify that your location is legal and safe to operate in. If you're flying under Part 107 (commercially), ensure you have the appropriate authorization for controlled airspace.

Next, monitor the weather. Drones are sensitive to wind, precipitation, and temperature extremes. Flying in poor conditions can drain your batteries quickly and affect GPS and camera performance.

Once on site, assess the launch and landing areas. Look for power lines, moving vehicles, people, animals, trees, or anything that might interfere with your flight path. Establish a clear line of sight and safe zones for both vertical and horizontal movement.

Finally, inspect your gear. Batteries, propellers, camera gimbals, and firmware all need to be in proper working order. Confirm all systems are updated, sensors are calibrated, and your controller is synced and charged.

With everything set, you're ready to fly confidently—and responsibly.

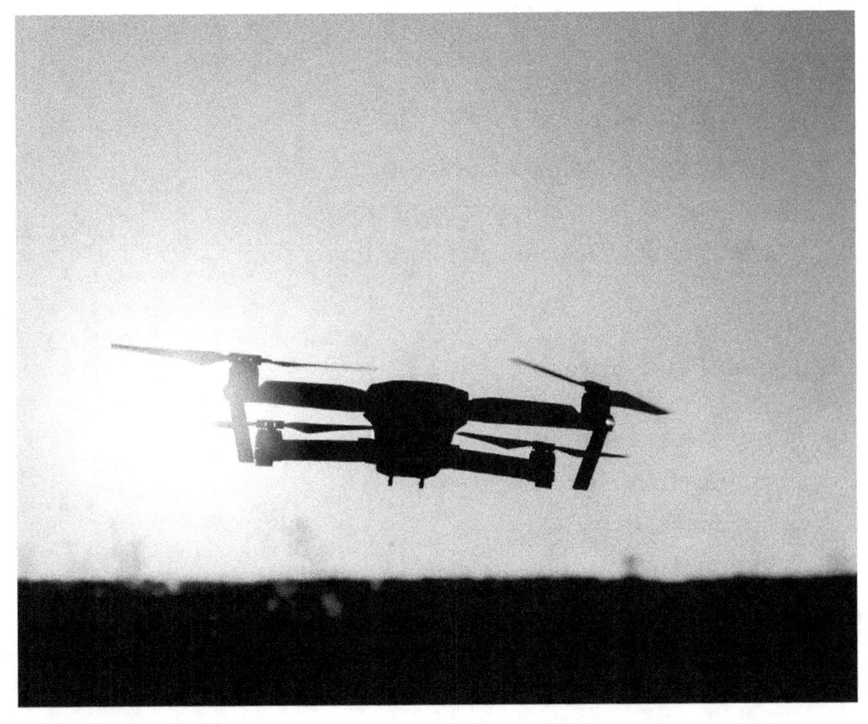

Pre-Flight Checklist for Drone Pilots

Use this checklist before every flight to make sure you're fully prepared.

Location and Legal

___ Confirm you're flying in legal airspace

___ Get FAA/LAANC authorization if required

___ Respect park and property rules

___ FAA Part 107 certificate and registration (if applicable)

Weather and Environment

___ Wind speed below 15 mph

___ No rain, fog, or snow

___ Clear visibility and favorable light

___ Temperature is within operational range

___ Avoid strong glare or sun in pilot's line of sight

Equipment and Power

___ Drone body and propellers are damage-free

___ Batteries fully charged and secured

___ Extra batteries packed

___ Remote controller is charged and functioning

___ SD card inserted with available space

___ Mobile device/app connected properly

System and Software

___ Firmware up to date

___ Compass and IMU calibrated (if needed)

___ GPS signal locked (8+ satellites)

___ Set Return-to-Home point and altitude

___ Camera settings configured for your mission

Site Safety

___ Launch/landing site is clear

___ No people, animals, or moving vehicles nearby

___ Obstacle scan completed (trees, power lines, buildings)

___ Maintain clear line of sight

___ Planned flight route and altitude reviewed

Pro Tip: Consider laminating your checklist or keeping it saved in your flight app so it's always ready. Routine pre-flight prep is one of the simplest ways to extend the life of your gear—and protect your drone from unnecessary risk.

NOTES

____

____

____

____

____

Chapter 7: Emergency Procedures

Drone flight emergencies can be intimidating, but knowing how to handle them can make all the difference in ensuring both your safety and the protection of your equipment. Here are some important emergency procedures to follow when faced with common drone issues like loss of signal, low battery warnings, and crashes.

Loss of Signal

One of the most common emergencies a drone pilot may encounter is a loss of signal between the drone and the remote control. This can happen due to interference, loss of range, or other technical problems. In this situation, the drone may automatically trigger a failsafe function, such as Return to Home (RTH). If this occurs, *"Wait for the drone to return to the home point (RTH)."* This ensures the drone will fly back to its takeoff location, avoiding further loss of control or an uncontrolled landing. If you can regain signal or control, *"Manually regain control if possible."* This will allow you to guide the drone safely back or correct its flight path. Always stay calm and use your judgment to determine whether it's safer to let the failsafe take over or manually regain control.

Battery Low Warning

Another emergency to be prepared for is a low battery warning. Drones typically send notifications when the battery is running low, but it's essential to monitor the battery levels throughout your flight. If you receive a low battery warning, you should *"Land immediately if below safe levels."* Avoid continuing the flight to capture that last shot or fly a little longer. A battery that dies mid-flight can lead to the drone falling out of the sky, causing potential damage or loss of the drone. Finding a safe landing area and bringing the drone down as soon as possible will prevent these risks and ensure you don't lose your drone unexpectedly.

Crash Protocol

Despite best efforts, crashes can sometimes happen. Whether it's a result of unexpected weather conditions, a sudden loss of control, or a technical malfunction, a crash can be a worrying situation. Once the drone has safely landed, *"Safely retrieve the drone."* Make sure to approach the drone cautiously, as it may still be hot or have spinning blades that can cause injury. Once you've safely recovered the drone, it's critical to *"Inspect for damage before the next flight."* Check for any physical damage to the propellers, camera, gimbal, or motors. Performing a thorough inspection ensures the drone is fully operational for its next flight and reduces the risk of another emergency occurring due to undetected issues.

Knowing your drone's emergency protocols and staying calm in these situations will allow you to handle most emergencies effectively. Always be prepared with a clear understanding of procedures for loss of signal, low battery warnings, and crash protocols, ensuring both your safety and the longevity of your drone.

NOTES

Chapter 8: Drone Maintenance Tips

Maintaining your drone is essential for ensuring its longevity, optimal performance, and safe operation. Regular drone maintenance not only helps prevent unexpected failures during flight but also ensures that your drone is always ready for the next adventure. Here are some key maintenance practices to keep your drone in top condition.

Cleaning Propellers and Motors

One of the simplest yet most important maintenance tasks is cleaning your drone's propellers and motors. During flight, debris such as dust, dirt, or grass can accumulate on these parts, affecting the drone's performance and stability. *"Regularly clean propellers and motors to remove debris."* A buildup of debris can cause vibrations, noise, or even damage the propellers, leading to a less efficient flight or, in severe cases, a crash. Use a soft brush or a microfiber cloth to gently remove any dirt or debris from these areas. Be sure to check the motors for any signs of wear or damage, and make sure they are spinning freely without any obstruction.

Battery Storage and Care

Your drone's battery is one of its most vital components, and proper battery care is crucial to extending its lifespan and maintaining flight performance. Storing your battery properly when not in use can make a significant difference in its longevity. *"Store batteries at a proper charge level (30%-50% for storage)."* Keeping your battery charged to this level ensures that it doesn't degrade over time and helps prevent issues like swelling or loss of charge capacity. If you plan to store your drone for an extended period, remove the battery from the drone and keep it in a cool, dry place. Avoid storing it in extreme temperatures, as this can damage the battery and reduce its overall lifespan.

Keeping Firmware and Apps Updated

Just like with any piece of technology, it's essential to keep your drone's firmware and companion apps updated. Manufacturers frequently release updates to improve performance, fix bugs, and ensure compatibility with new features or software. *"Keep firmware and apps updated to the latest versions."* Regularly check for firmware updates for both your drone and its remote controller. These updates can provide improvements to flight stability, GPS accuracy, and battery management. Similarly, updating the companion app ensures that you have access to the latest features and settings, allowing you to control the drone more effectively and take advantage of any new functionalities.

In addition to these key maintenance tips, always ensure that your drone's body and gimbal are free from damage and debris, and check for any loose parts before each flight.

It's also a good practice to conduct a pre-flight inspection, verifying that all components are functioning correctly. By staying on top of these maintenance tasks, you'll increase the lifespan of your drone and improve its performance, ensuring that you can enjoy smooth, trouble-free flights for years to come.

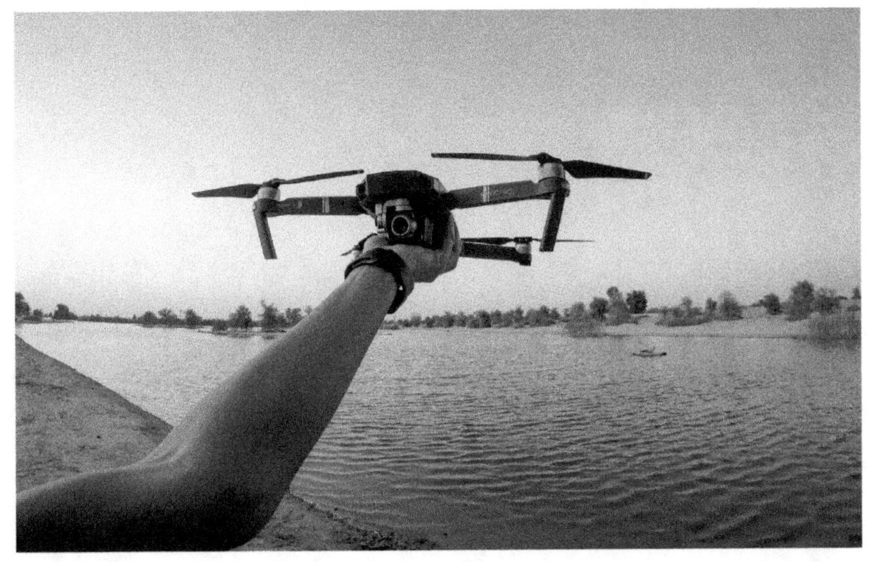

Chapter 9: Quick Tips for Success

Flying a drone can be an incredibly rewarding experience, whether you're using it for photography, mapping, or simply exploring the skies. However, like any other skill, it requires practice, patience, and an understanding of best practices to ensure success and safety.

Here are some quick tips to help you get the most out of your drone flying experience.

1. Start in Open Spaces with Minimal Obstacles

When you're just starting, it's important to practice in a safe environment where you can focus on learning how to control the drone without the added stress of navigating around obstacles. *"Start in open spaces with minimal obstacles."* Large, open fields or clearings are ideal for beginners because they allow you to practice hovering, flying, and controlling the drone without the risk of crashing into trees, buildings, or other objects.

This also gives you plenty of room to make mistakes and learn from them without causing damage to your drone. As you gain confidence, you can gradually move to more complex environments with trees, structures, or other potential hazards.

2. Practice Emergency Landings Regularly

Emergencies can arise when flying drones, such as signal loss, battery issues, or even unexpected weather changes. One of the most important skills you can develop is the ability to land your drone safely in emergency situations. *"Practice emergency landings regularly."* Set aside time during each flight to intentionally simulate a scenario where you must land quickly. Whether you're practicing a low battery warning or signal loss, knowing how to perform a controlled emergency landing will help you react calmly and effectively if something goes wrong. It's also helpful to become familiar with your drone's failsafe functions, such as Return to Home (RTH), which will automatically return the drone to its launch point in the event of a lost signal or low battery. Practicing this skill will ensure that, in an emergency, you can make quick decisions that minimize risk and damage to your drone.

3. Log Flight Hours to Track Your Experience and Improve Skills

Like any other skill, the more you practice flying your drone, the better you'll become. One of the best ways to track your progress and identify areas for improvement is to *"Log flight hours to track your experience and improve skills."* Keeping a log allows you to note the conditions of each flight, such as weather, location, flight time, and any challenges you faced.

Over time, this will help you see how much progress you've made and highlight areas where you might need more practice. You can also use the log to set goals for your flying, such as working on specific maneuvers or mastering advanced features like camera settings or automated flight paths. Logging your flight hours also provides a valuable record for maintenance, as you can track the number of flights and total hours on your drone, which can help you schedule necessary maintenance or repairs.

4. Familiarize Yourself with Local Regulations

Before flying your drone, it's crucial to be aware of the local laws and regulations governing drone flights. Different countries and regions have varying rules regarding where and when you can fly, as well as requirements for registering your drone or obtaining a drone pilot's license. Make sure you're familiar with these regulations to avoid any legal trouble or fines. Many areas have designated no-fly zones, particularly near airports, government buildings, or large crowds. Always check airspace restrictions and avoid flying in prohibited zones.

5. Understand Your Drone's Features and Settings

Each drone model comes with its own set of features, such as altitude limits, geofencing, GPS tracking, and intelligent flight modes. Understanding how these features work and how to customize them will help you fly your drone more effectively. For example, many drones have an automatic return feature when battery levels are low or signal is lost. These settings can vary between models, so it's essential to read the manual thoroughly and experiment with different flight modes to understand the full capabilities of your drone.

6. Use the Right Flight Techniques

Good flying techniques not only enhance your control but also ensure that your drone remains stable and efficient during flight. Always keep the drone's propellers facing forward when flying and avoid abrupt movements that could throw the drone off balance. Smooth, gradual throttle adjustments are key to controlling altitude and speed. If you're flying in windy conditions, keep the drone close to the ground until you are confident in handling it, as wind resistance can affect your control.

7. Stay Calm and Focused

Flying a drone can be exhilarating, but it's important to remain calm and focused during the flight. Whether you're dealing with an unexpected gust of wind, a signal interruption, or simply learning the controls, staying calm will allow you to make better decisions. Always keep your attention on the drone and its surroundings, avoiding distractions. If you find yourself feeling overwhelmed, it's okay to take a break and try again later.

Successful drone flying comes down to practice, awareness, and a focus on safety. By starting in open spaces, practicing emergency landings, logging flight hours, and familiarizing yourself with local regulations and drone features, you'll be well on your way to becoming a skilled and confident drone pilot. Keep honing your skills, and remember that each flight, whether successful or not, is a valuable opportunity to learn and improve.

NOTES

Chapter 10: Basic Drone Photography and Videography Tips

Drone photography and videography have become increasingly popular as they offer a unique perspective and stunning aerial shots that are impossible to achieve with traditional photography equipment. With advancements in drone technology, even beginner drone pilots can capture breathtaking images and videos. Whether you're looking to shoot a sweeping landscape, film an event, or create cinematic visuals, understanding the basics of drone photography and videography is essential to achieving professional-looking results. Here's a guide to get you started.

Understanding the Basics of Drone Photography and Videography

Before diving into shooting, it's important to understand a few core principles that will help you capture better shots. Drone photography is more than just sending a camera into the sky—it requires thoughtful planning, technical knowledge, and an eye for composition. Key factors such as lighting, altitude, camera settings, and flight stability play a major role in determining the quality of your images. Understanding how to frame a shot from above, balance exposure in changing light conditions, and follow local airspace regulations ensures not only visually compelling results but also safe and responsible flying. By learning these fundamentals before takeoff, you'll be better equipped to transform ordinary scenes into breathtaking aerial images.

Know Your Drone's Capabilities

Different drones have varying levels of performance, from basic models to professional-grade ones with advanced camera systems. Make sure you're familiar with your drone's camera specifications, such as resolution, frame rate, ISO, and shutter speed. The more you know, the better you can adjust settings for different conditions and effects. For instance, some drones, like those from DJI, allow you to shoot in various formats like JPEG or RAW for photos and 4K or 1080p for video.

Lighting

Lighting is one of the most important factors in photography and videography. Natural light plays a significant role in the quality of your shots. Golden hour—early morning or late afternoon—provides soft, diffused light that can dramatically enhance your shots. Avoid shooting in harsh midday sunlight, as it can create overexposed areas and unappealing shadows.

Stability and Smooth Movements

Smooth, stable footage is crucial for good drone videography. Unstable movements or shaky footage can ruin the effect of a cinematic shot. When flying, focus on keeping your drone movements slow and deliberate. Use the drone's smooth flight mode to help with this. Additionally, many drones are equipped with gimbals to stabilize the camera, ensuring smoother footage even during turbulent conditions.

Composition

As with traditional photography, the composition of your shot is key. Follow basic composition rules like the rule of thirds, leading lines, and framing to make your images visually appealing. Aerial shots often benefit from showing the relationship between the subject and the surrounding environment, so be mindful of the environment you're capturing.

Using Mastershots on DJI Drones

One of the standout features of modern DJI drones, like the DJI Air 2S, Mavic Air 2, and Mini 2, is the ability to capture dynamic, cinematic footage with minimal effort through the use of "Mastershots." Master-shots are automated flight paths that allow you to capture professional-grade videos with a single press of a button. They are an excellent tool for beginners who want to create impressive videos without needing extensive piloting skills.

How to Use Mastershots on DJI Drones:

Preparation
Before starting the Mastershot, ensure your drone is in an open space with minimal obstacles. Check the battery levels and GPS signal to ensure a stable flight. Also, verify that your camera settings are optimal for the shooting conditions—set the resolution and frame rate according to your needs.

Select the Subject
Mastershots are designed to focus on a specific subject, so choose the subject you want the drone to track. You can either manually select it on the screen or let the drone detect it automatically. This feature is particularly useful for filming people, objects, or landmarks.

Activate Mastershots
Once you've chosen your subject, open the DJI app and select the "Mastershots" option in the flight menu. You'll be prompted to choose the type of shot you want to capture. DJI drones offer various predefined flight paths, including:

> **Rocket:** The drone ascends vertically, providing a high-angle view of the subject.
> **Dolly Zoom:** The camera zooms in while the drone moves backward, creating the effect of a dynamic perspective change.
> **Circle:** The drone orbits around the subject, creating a smooth circular motion.
> **Helix:** A combination of upward and outward spiraling motion around the subject for dramatic, 360-degree coverage.
> **Parallax:** The drone moves sideways while maintaining focus on the subject, resulting in a perspective shift.

Start the Shot

Once you've chosen the desired Mastershot, press the "Start" button. The drone will automatically take off, fly along the preset path, and capture footage according to the selected pattern. During the Mastershot, you can adjust the altitude, distance, and other parameters, but the drone will handle the basic flight and filming.

Review and Adjust

After the Mastershot is completed, review the footage on the DJI app. Most drones will provide a preview of the shots so you can determine if the sequence needs to be retaken. If you're not satisfied with the result, adjust the settings or select a different Mastershot mode for a varied perspective.

Post-Processing

Once you have your footage, you can use editing software to fine-tune the video, adjust color grading, add music, and make any necessary cuts. DJI drones typically offer high-quality video output, so with good editing, you can create professional-looking content.

Additional Tips for Better Drone Photography and Videography

Use ND Filters

Neutral density (ND) filters help to reduce the amount of light entering the camera lens, which is especially useful in bright conditions. ND filters allow you to slow down the shutter speed, achieving smoother, more cinematic footage. They are particularly important for drone videography as they help prevent overexposure and keep the video looking natural.

Avoid High Wind Conditions

Wind can significantly affect both drone stability and camera quality. High winds can cause the drone to shake or drift, resulting in shaky footage or difficulty controlling the drone. Always check weather conditions before flying, and avoid flying in gusty or turbulent weather.

Experiment with Angles

Try different camera angles to add variety to your shots. Low-angle shots can emphasize the size of the subject, while higher angles provide a grander perspective of the surrounding landscape. Moving the drone along a curved flight path or using the gimbal to adjust the tilt can also help create more engaging footage.

Maintain Battery Life

Always be mindful of your drone's battery life. Plan your flights to ensure you have enough time to return to the launch point safely. Avoid pushing the drone too far from its home point if the battery is running low, as this can result in an emergency landing.

Mastering drone photography and videography takes time and practice, but with the right equipment and techniques, you can capture stunning visuals from the sky. By understanding the basics—lighting, composition, and smooth movements—and utilizing powerful features like DJI's Mastershots, even beginners can create professional-grade content. Regularly practicing your flying skills and exploring creative ways to film will help you improve and make the most out of your drone's capabilities.

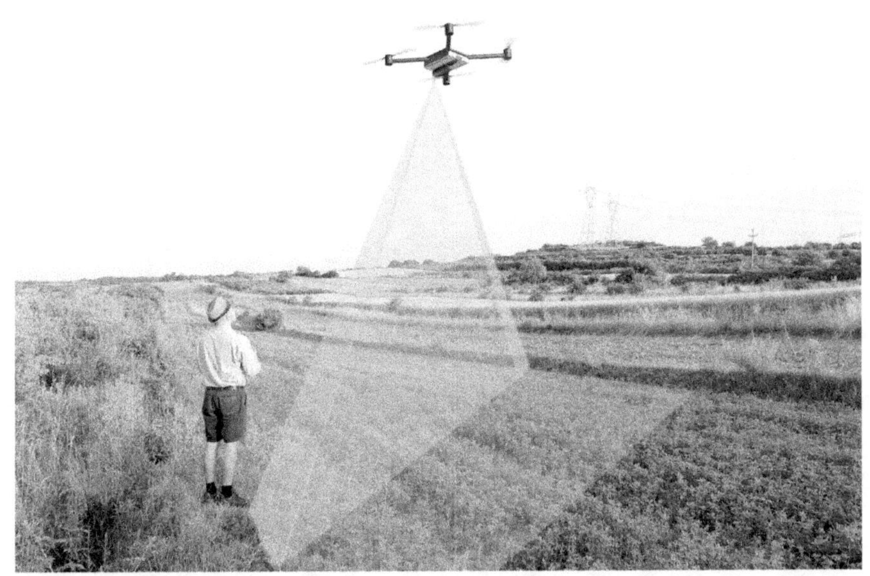

Conclusion

As you continue your journey through the skies, remember that the best pilots are those who never stop learning, stay curious, and fly with both confidence and care. Whether you're mapping farmland, filming stunning aerial videos, or simply enjoying a quiet flight at sunset, your drone is a powerful tool—and this guide is here to help you use it wisely.

Keep this pocket guide handy for quick references in the field, pre-flight checks, or a fast refresher when planning your next mission. And above all, fly safe, fly smart, and enjoy every second above the ground.

Clear skies and happy flying!

Visuals for Quick Reference

Drone and Controller Example (DJI Mini Pro 4 model)

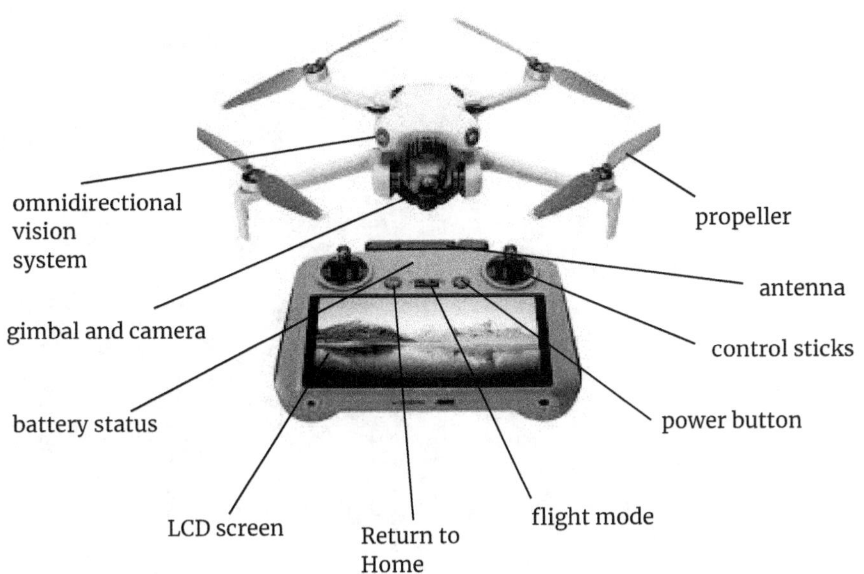

Find the DJI Mini Pro 4 Drone User Manual here

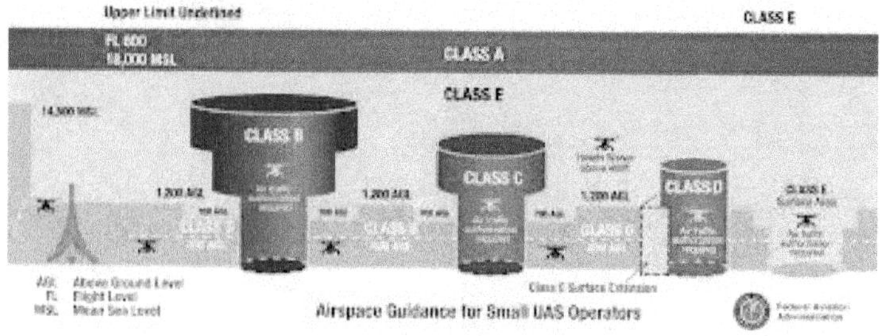

<u>FAA Air Space Classifications</u>
<u>https://www.faa.gov/uas/</u>

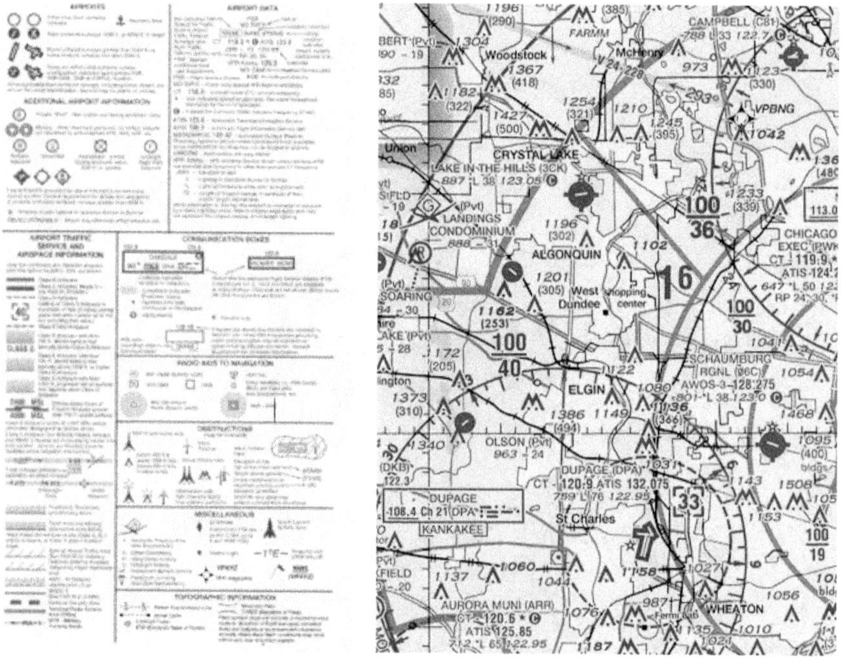

<u>FAA Aeronautical Section Chart and Legend</u>
<u>https://www.faa.gov/air_traffic/flight_info/aeronav/productcatalog/vfrcharts/sectional/</u>

NOTES

Additional Drone Resources

Websites

FAA – UAS Drone Zone

https://faadronezone-access.faa.gov

 – Register your drone, apply for waivers, file incident reports, and access Part 107 info.

FAA – Remote Pilot Certificate (Part 107)

https://www.faa.gov/uas/commercial_operators/

 – Study materials, testing center locations, renewal details.

B4UFLY App

https://www.faa.gov/uas/getting_started/b4ufly

 – FAA's app to check if it's safe and legal to fly in your area.

LAANC Authorization System

https://www.faa.gov/uas/programs_partnerships/data_exchange

 – Get near real-time airspace approvals.

DJI Mini Pro 4 User Manual

https://dl.djicdn.com/downloads/DJI_Mini_4_Pro/DJI_Mini_4_Pro_User_Manual_EN.pdf

-Find instructions for drone use, diagrams and troubleshooting tips.

Courses

Pilot Institute - Part 107 Made Easy
https://www.pilotinstitute.com
 – Register your drone, apply for waivers, file incident reports, and access Part 107 info.

Drone Pilot Ground School
https://www.dronepilotgroundschool.com
 – Comprehensive Part 107 prep with practice tests, videos, and lifetime access

UAV Coach – Part 107 Exam Prep
https://www.uavcoach.com/part107-test-prep
 – Video-based learning, bonus airspace and night flying modules.

Remote Pilot 101
https://remotepilot101.com
 – Easy-to-digest video modules, regularly updated to reflect new FAA rules.

Apps and Tools for Flying

AirMap
https://www.airmap.com

Know Before You Fly
https://knowbeforeyoufly.org

Check out the link below for your additional free,
printable POCKET PILOT Drone Checklists!

https://drive.google.com/drive/folders/1Y3KZOOwgjyxanZork
XdQCweWaS-XtEns?usp=drive_link

Studying for the Part 107 Drone Certification Test?

Scan the QR for my favorite Part 107 drone certification test study resources playlist on YouTube.

NOTES

Glossary

Aerial Photography

Capturing images or video from an elevated position using a drone, offering perspectives not achievable from the ground.

Altitude

The height of the drone above ground level or sea level. Most drones have altitude limits based on local regulations.

Auto Exposure (AE)

A camera setting that automatically adjusts exposure based on lighting conditions to produce a well-lit image.

Auto White Balance (AWB)

A feature that automatically adjusts the white balance to ensure colors look natural under different lighting.

Cinematic Mode

A flight mode that smooths out drone movements for fluid, movie-like footage.

Dynamic Range

The range of light levels a camera sensor can capture, from darkest shadows to brightest highlights. A higher dynamic range allows better detail in challenging light.

Electronic Image Stabilization (EIS)

A digital method to reduce camera shake in video by adjusting frames after capturing.

First-Person View (FPV)

A live video feed from the drone's camera, displayed on a mobile device, headset, or controller screen, giving the pilot a "from the sky" view.

Frame Rate (FPS)

Frames per second — the number of images captured per second in a video. Common drone FPS rates include 24, 30, or 60 fps.

Gimbal

A mechanical stabilizer that holds the drone's camera steady during flight, allowing smooth footage even in windy conditions.

Geo-Fencing

A virtual boundary that prevents the drone from flying into restricted or dangerous areas (like airports or no-fly zones).

GPS Mode

A flight mode that uses satellite signals to maintain position and altitude, making the drone easier to control and hover.

HDR (High Dynamic Range)

A photography technique combining multiple exposures to create one image with better details in highlights and shadows.

ISO

A camera setting that controls the sensor's sensitivity to light. Higher ISO can brighten dark scenes but may add grain or noise.

Manual Mode

A camera mode where you manually adjust exposure, shutter speed, ISO, and other settings for creative control.

Mastershots

An intelligent DJI flight feature that performs a sequence of automated movements while capturing video of a subject from multiple angles, then compiles it into a cinematic video.

ND Filter (Neutral Density Filter)

A lens filter that reduces the amount of light entering the camera, allowing slower shutter speeds or wider apertures for better video quality.

Obstacle Avoidance

Sensors on the drone that detect and help avoid objects in its flight path to prevent collisions.

Orbit/Point of Interest Mode

An intelligent flight mode where the drone circles around a selected subject while keeping the camera focused on it.

RAW Format

An uncompressed image file format that retains all sensor data, allowing more flexibility in editing compared to JPEG.

RTH (Return to Home)

A safety feature that automatically flies the drone back to its takeoff point in case of signal loss or low battery.

Shutter Speed

The length of time the camera's shutter is open. Slower speeds create motion blur; faster speeds freeze motion.

Telemetry

Live data transmitted from the drone to the controller, including altitude, battery life, distance, and GPS status.

Three-Axis Gimbal

A type of gimbal that stabilizes the camera on three axes — pitch, roll, and yaw — for ultra-smooth video.

Waypoints

A flight path planning feature where users set specific GPS points for the drone to follow automatically.

www.ingramcontent.com/pod-product-compliance
Lightning Source LLC
Chambersburg PA
CBHW061042050726
47592CB00004B/1554